WOLVEY LOC/

OLD PHOTOGRAPHS
FROM THE VILLAGES

A selection of historic photographs
from the Warwickshire villages of
BURTON HASTINGS
COPSTON MAGNA
WITHYBROOK
WOLVEY

Published by
Wolvey Local History Group
Wolvey · Warwickshire
England
www.wolvey-history.org.uk

First Edition, 2004

ISBN: 0-9546751-0-X

Text, design and typesetting by members of the
Wolvey Local History Group · Warwickshire
Printed by RCS plc, Retford

Cover: The Galliford Bus with local school children. part of the procession to celebrate the 50th anniversary of VJ (Victory in Japan) Day in 1996. There were street parties and a service in Wolvey Church, lead by Mr D A Lamb, himself an ex-Japanese prisioner-of-war.

CONTENTS

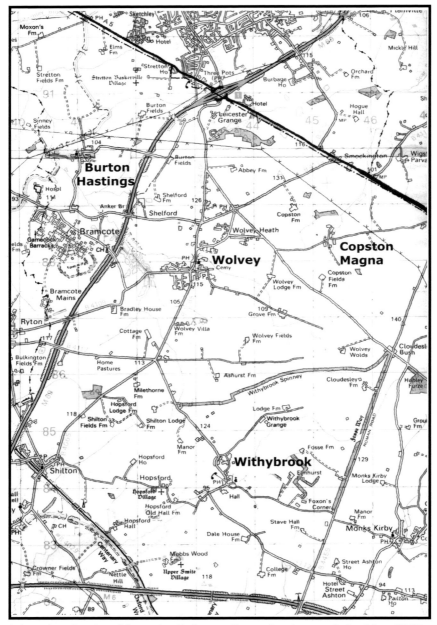

Adapted and reduced from the Ordnance Survey Landranger Series Map, 2002 (Sheet 140)

Introduction

THE WOLVEY LOCAL HISTORY GROUP draws its membership from the villages of Burton Hastings, Copston Magna, Withybrook and Wolvey. All of them have medieval or earlier origins. Today they share the same Vicar and, except Withybrook, the same School.

For over 4,000 years people have lived in the area. Flint tools dating to Neolithic times and Bronze Age burial mounds are to be found on Wolvey Heath.   Iron Age farmers almost certainly tilled the soil and trudged along the Fosse Way, eventually to become a Roman road linking modern Devon with Lincolnshire. This and Watling Street, the Roman road connecting London and the south-east with Wales, cross in the area at High Cross where the Roman settlement of Venonis existed. Evidence suggesting a Roman villa has been found at Copston Magna. By the ninth century, in the time of King Alfred, Watling Street formed the boundary with the Danes.

It is about this time that the nucleus of the present villages begin to form. Certainly when the Domesday Book was compiled in 1086, the villages of Burton Hastings and Wolvey (with Bramcote) are in existence as well as two villages that ceased in medieval times at Stretton Baskerville and Hopsford because of the Black Death and changes in farming practice from arable to sheep. The presence of priests at Burton Hastings and Wolvey suggests churches in both places; a mill was recorded at Burton Hastings. During the middle ages Wolvey was granted a fair and weekly market. The enclosures of the eighteenth century transformed the landscape from large open fields into the pattern of fields which until recently were a feature of the local countryside.

From the late nineteenth century, part of the story of our villages can be told from photographs. A few of the photographs in this book were taken by professional photographers, mainly for the local press, but the majority were taken by people living in the villages and have been lent for copying and inclusion in the Group's photographic archive. It is as a result of that archive and with the help of many villagers, past and present, that the Wolvey Local History Group has been able to publish this book. We also acknowledge with thanks a gift from GallifordTry plc towards the cost of printing this publication.

Farm labourer at Wolvey, 1896

PLACES OF WORSHIP

By Norman times we know of churches at Wolvey and Burton Hastings. By 1400 there was also a church at Stretton Baskerville. Copston and the new church at Withybrook were chapels attached to the large church at Monks Kirby. This arrangement continued until recent times. When Henry VIII broke the church away from Rome, Stretton Baskerville was in ruins, the parish joining with Burton Hastings. With the advent of nonconformism, chapels were established at Burton, Wolvey and Withybrook. Late in the nineteenth century a catholic chapel was built at Wolvey Hall, to be replaced by a church on Coventry Road. The most recent place of worship is an interdenominational chapel and temple for Gurkha soldiers and their families at Bramcote Barracks.

Wolvey Church, circa 1820.   In an extensive restoration in the late nineteenth century, the chancel was virtually rebuilt in the 'Gothic style' and the nave gained a higher roof and new clerestory windows

Wolvey Church, 1953. The new porch was built in 1909. The graveyard has been tidied up with many of the tombstones laid flat to aid grass mowing. In 1962 and in 1963 a mower was won as first prize for the best kept Warwickshire churchyard,

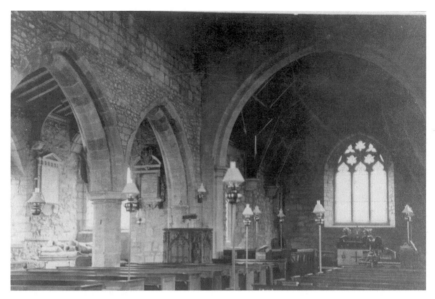

Interior of Wolvey Church, 1900, following a years's closure for restoration work. Oil lamps are still in use, and there is a new pulpit on the left of the chancel arch. There is no organ to obscure the tombs at the end of the north aisle.

East end of Wolvey Church during the 1950's. The pulpit is now on the right of the chancel arch and a new organ obscures the north aisle. Behind the altar is a new reredos, a memorial to those who died during the First World War.

THE OLD VICARAGE, WOLVEY.   L.J.M

A drawing of the old vicarage at Wolvey. This building was replaced by the house below. During the Middle Ages the church was served by the monks of Coombe Abbey. Later the vicars were prebends from Lichfield Cathedral, where there is a Wolvey stall

Wolvey Vicarage, 1896. The new vicar, the Rev William Bleiben (1896-1905) stands in front of the house with his family. The house was demolished and in 1972 replaced by the present vicarage and a close with four houses.

Ladies of the Mothers' Union having tea in the orchard of the old vicarage. Its large garden and beautiful trees stretched from Church Hill to School Lane and was a regular venue for the Mothers' Union tea party. In 1956 a Bring and Buy stall and charges for tea raised £12 10s.
Seated l to r: Eunice Elliot; Mary Middleton; Jinny Allen; Doris Joyce; Ruby Malin; Lizzie Bennet; Edie Bailey.

Choir, Wolvey Church, 1955-1960.
l to r: Rev Hudson; Olive York; Bill Thorpe; Agnes Beale; Mr Riley; Wilma Thorpe; Derek Woodward; Jill Hood; Ethel York; Freda Hood; Mrs Hudson. Front row: Jim Chase; Bill Chase; Janet Castell; Doreen Weller; Aron Widdow.

The Burton Hastings Church Bells, 1937 after their renovation. The tenor bell was recast and two new bells added to complete the ring of five. The work was done at Taylor's Bellfoundry, Loughborough.

Bellringers of Burton Hastings Church, late 1930s.
left to right:
Bill Chamberlain, Arthur Plowman, Tom Wilson;
At back:
Bill Bark, Jack Morris, George Callington, Bill Noon.

Burton Hastings Church. This view shows an earlier porch, replaced in 1915. The young Scot's pines have guards to protect them from grazing sheep.

Interior of Burton Hastings Church. St Botolph's Church lit by oil lamps. Only one of these survived when electricity was installed in 1937. The pews were replaced by 80 chairs in 1915.

Christmas Day bread distribution.
Both Burton Hastings and Wolvey have a charity which distributes bread to parishioners who attend the Christmas Service. Here worshippers at Burton Hastings are seen leaving the church with their loaves of bread.
Left to right:
Major Atkins, Mrs Wells, Mr Ward, Mr Arthur Plowman, (?) , Mrs Kath Chamberlain, Miss Barbara Elson, Mrs Plowman, Mrs M Callington.

Burton Hastings school children 1960. *The Rev Gibbons welcomes children from Burton Hastings school with their headteacher, Mrs Elsie Wells. They processed from the school to the church, carrying their gifts, twice a year for the flower and harvest festivals.*

Copston Magna churchyard. The celebration of the silver jubilee of King George V in 1935. The Rev Peacock is planting one of the trees presented by Mr Percy Goodwin in memory of his daughter Mary.

The Rev A R Jones, Vicar of Monks Kirby, 1949-59. Copston Magna church, in the background, was at that time a Chapel of Ease of Monks Kirby parish.

Withybrook Church. A newspaper article of 1891 mentioned a huge weathercock, leaning so far that it would soon fall. The present smaller weather-cock is part of the restoration that saved the church. In 1954, as a result of three feet of flooding in the lane to the church, the harvest festival service was postponed.

Withybrook Church central aisle, August 1891. In 1889 the roof was in such a bad state of repair that during a sermon most of the rain fell on the Vicar. As a result, services were held in the school. The church was abandoned to the bats. Articles in the *Birmingham Daily Gazette* commented on the disgraceful state of the church. Plans were drawn up to restore the church at a cost of £1,250. The population of the village was only 234. Most of the money raised came from outside the parish including one donation from New Zealand.

Withybrook Chapel
At the top of the lane is the Independent Chapel, built in 1843; on the left is the roof of the manse. There was a Sunday School. Once a year, after 'sermons', a supper was held in the school room. The last burial was in 1940. The manse was demolished in 1965.

Burton Hastings Chapel. Now demolished, it can be seen here at the end of the row of cottages in Cicey (sometimes Cecily) Lane. Ron Brandrick with his bike is in the foreground with his mother, Mary in the doorway.

Wolvey Baptist Chapel congregation, photographed in the chapel yard, 1900. Membership was about 50 at this time but had reached 80 in 1870.

Wolvey Baptist Sunday School, 1930s. The children, in their Sunday best clothes are with their teachers, Ted Joyce, Mary Dalton, Ken Pullen, Elsie Harrison and Rennie Lucas. Also in the photograph are Meg Osburn, Frank Middleton, Joan Yorke and Doreen Peryn. Founded in 1804, a school room was added to the chapel in 1818 and extended at a cost of £87 in 1856 due to 'a considerably enlarged population'. In 1967, 60 children attended, the older ones meeting upstairs and the younger ones downstairs.

Wolvey Baptist Lay Pastor, Mr A Grinham(on left) with his wife and Mr Malin on an outing to Skegness. During the week he was a manager on the night shift at the 'Humber' - a Coventry carworks. The first preacher, George Toone, opened his house for preaching in 1768. The chapel was built in 1789 but at first church membership remained with Hinckley Baptist Chapel. In 1815 they were able to pay their own minister £30 a year. There has been no full-time pastor since 1915.

Harvest Festival, Wolvey Baptist Chapel, 1950s. Thanksgiving for a good harvest is always important in a country village. The children brought gifts of home-grown produce which were distributed to the sick and aged. The remainder was sold on the Monday. With the collection, some £26 was raised.

Catholic Chapel, Wolvey Hall. Built in 1890 by H F J Coape-Arnold who is seen here with his wife Mary Genevieve and five of his twelve children.

Interior of Catholic Chapel, Wolvey Hall. Designed in the Gothic style, it had seats for ninety. It was replaced in 1924 by the Church of St James the Less in Coventry Road.

Left:
Stanley Ward, born in August 1910. Dedicated at Wolvey Baptist Chapel, 1911.

Right:
Baptism of Kristie Thorpe in Wolvey Church 1993 by Rev Ray James, Vicar of the parishes of Wolvey, Burton Hastings with Stretton Baskerville, Copston Magna and Withybrook.

EDUCATION

Until the nineteenth century most of the villagers would have received no formal education. Generally, children would have learned from their parents and been required to work from an early age. Some boys might have received education in the monasteries before their dissolution by Henry VIII. Grammar schools were established at Nuneaton and Coventry in the sixteenth century but these were only for a few boys. The rich could afford private tutors. Sometimes parsons would teach pupils in their own homes.

Certainly the church brought education to the villages. In the mid-eighteenth century the Vicar of Wolvey ran a Boarding Academy for young gentlemen. His successor, appointed in 1784 quickly established a Charity School for poor children. A Sunday school ran in parallel with this. In 1811 a Wolvey Weekly Charity School was formed. Although government legislation in 1833 made state grants available for schools, these do not seem to have been sought in the villages before mid-century. When they were the schools became national schools and subject to inspection..

Wolvey School girls, 1896
Left to right:
back row: Ada Lines, Bessie Smith, (?) , Eliza Allcoat, Polly Upton, Lillie Birchall, Gertie Bark, Mary Elizabeth Knight , (?). front row: (?) . Madge Elliott, Alice Kenny.

In addition to normal lessons, the girls also did needlework. In September 1896 all the pupils were invited by Mr Coape-Arnold for tea. They received gifts of toys, sweets, nuts, pence and fruit and had races and games on the cricket field.

Wolvey School boys, 1896
Left to right:
back row: (?) , (?) , (?) , Thomas Dewis; front row: Harry Oakes, (?) , (?) ,, [Policeman's son], Sid Allroat, Cecil Malin,---- Barnes, Albert Upton, (?) (?).

The School Log Book for 1896 mentions absenteeism in June on account of parents keeping their children back to pick peas, despite two vacations of two weeks for pea picking and harvest. At this time there were 96 pupils at the school. In addition to reading, writing and arithmatic, they had music lessons, being taught a new song *The whistling farmer's boy.*

Main classroom, old Wolvey School, 1900s. Forty-three children, the girls in starched pinafores and the boys collars and ties. One of the duties of the school monitor was to mix the ink and fill the ink wells, which can be seen in the desks.

Wolvey Night School, 1897. In the centre are Francis Seaton and his wife, Helen de Vere Seaton. He had been appointed in January as headteacher of the village school and stayed until 1925; his wife was an infant teacher until her early death in 1908. The night school started in 1893 and survived until 1913 when attendances fell because so many of the youth of the village were working in factories in Hinckley and Burbage. There were 48 scholars in 1897, studying such subjects as geography (illustrated with lantern slides), physiology as well as reading, writing and arithmatic.

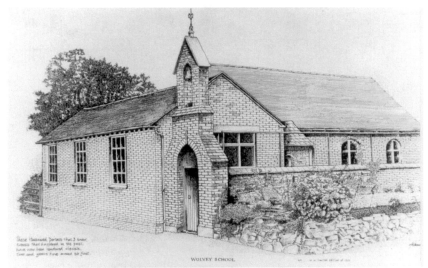

The old Wolvey School (drawing by Alan Warner). The school was first built in 1837 for the Sunday School. In the 1840s it was also used as a day school for infants. When it became a national (church) school about 1850, a small extension was added, the infants using this with the older children in the main room. A playground was added at the same time. With the growth of the school to 99 pupils in 1869, a new large room was added. A kitchen extension in June 1949 served 50 Wolvey pupils and those at Burton Hastings and Withybrook schools. Above the door can be seen the arch for the school bell, all that now remains of the old school, following its move to Bulkington Road in 1973.

School toilets (below).These replaced the earth closets installed in the playground in 1869. There was a separate block for boys and girls.

Retirement of Carl Beck, Headteacher of Wolvey School, 1935 - 1973.

Left to right:

Front row: Roger Moore, Adam Lea, Terence Miles, Hayley Crane, Stephen Wilson, Jonathan Preece, Dawn Longdon, Penny Ashfield, Rosalie Moore, Diane White, Elaine York, Dawn Wootton, David Morley, Sarah Patterson, Elaine Jackson, Clive Percival, Karen Sambell, Helen Patterson, Jon Farren, Garry Coupland, Tracey Harrison, Tracey Farren, Adrian Warwick, Jane Longdon, Ian Brown.

Second row: Stephen Newman, Gary Woolley, Neil Jackson, Miss Stratford, Mrs E Wrightham, Mrs C Clarke, Mrs N Hood, Mrs M West Mr L C Beck, Mrs J Compton, Mrs J Thorpe, Miss M Turvill, Mrs D Clarke, Mrs I Hurley, Richard Brown, Mark Timson, Robert Moore, Richard Newman.

Third row: Helen Fletcher, Victoria Brown, Neil Fletcher, Michael Castelle, John Kinchin, Paul Arnold, Grayson Percival, Andrew Castelle, Alan Jackson, David Randle, Karen Warner, Peter Boulton, Gerald Addison, Michelle Hurley, Richard Clarke, Sally Flowers.

Back row: Alan Wilson, Robin Moore, Kevan Moore, Nigel Jackson, Gaynor Moore, Valerie Griffiths, Stephen Smith, Pauline Brophy, Susan Isaac, Jane Moore, Joanne Thorpe, Sharon Furborough, Joanna Smith, Pearl Lewis.

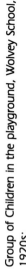

Group of Children in the playground, Wolvey School, 1920s;

Left to right:

Back row: Joe Moore, Mavis Clarke, Beryl Saunders, Beattie Whitton, Tom Bailey, (?) , Nora Chinn, Chrissie Thompson, Doris Moore, David Blackhall.

Middle row: Norman Moore, Bill York, (?) , Bill Bennett, Gladys Moore, (?) , Douglas Sowerby, (?) , Mary Sutton, (?) , Kath Moore, (?) , Ted Wilcocks.

Front row: Jim Brophy, Alan Watson, John Cleaver, Jack Williams, Betty York, (?) , (?) , Bill Bazely, Morris Bazely.

Burton Hastings School, 1960s. The mobile classroom was erected in 2 - 3 days according to the entry in the school log book fror 15 January 1958 and was used for infant children. It was needed to accommodate the children of servicemen from Bramcote Barracks.

Old School House, Burton Hastings. Outside stands 'Granny Cook'. A number of children received their education here, adjacent to Drag Lane, prior to the founding of the village school.

Burton Hastings School photograph, 1930s.
Left to right:
Back row: Don Francis, Edward Smith, Percy Morris, Fred Bull, Jim Gomm, Fred Cook, Harry Raven, Fred Lan, George Callington, Sam Smith, Billy Law, Mrs Goodall.
Middle row: Betty Cook, Doris Noon, Edie Plowman, Doll Ward, Nell Bull, Loie Wilson, Cath Brown, Olive Goodacre, Matilda Raven, Dolly Hyatt, Jenny Wilson.
Front row: ---- Fennick, Mary Chamberlain, Hetty Raven, Joan Furniss, Gladys Bradshaw, Wendy Law, Rene Wilson, Edith Ward, Liz Gomm, Stella Morris.

Burton Hastings School garden. The old school house is in the background.
Left to right:
Stella Morris, Joan Furness, Kath Brown, Doris Noon, Matilda Raven, Helen Raven, Lizzie Gomm.

Maypole Dancing, Burton Hastings School, early 1950s. Rehearsing in the school playground, ready for the school fête.

Fancy Dress Parade, Burton Hastings School. Old lady (side view) Hannah Brandrick; Boy and girl (in front) Tommy and Eunice Upton; Boy (behind cowboy) Frank Miller; Man (behind little girl in centre) Brian Tipper; Boy in kilt: John Harvey.

Burton Hastings School Staff.
Back row (left to right): Mrs Chamberlain (Caretaker), Mrs Plowman (Housekeeper),
Stella Young (Dinner Lady), May Freeman (Dinner Lady).
Front row: Mrs Middleton (Infant Teacher), Mrs Wells (Headteacher)

Banner for Consecration of Coventry Cathedral, 1 June 1962. Joan King and Suzanne
Callington with the banner they are to carry, representing the Church of St Botolph,
Burton Hastings. The banner was made by Mrs Wells and Mr R W Young.

Village School Withybrook, 1920s. The school was opened in 1856 as a Church of England school with two classrooms in the Main Street. The headteacher and his wife live in the school house alongside. There were about 50 pupils in the 1920s. The school closed in 1956 with children having to travel to Monks Kirby

Withybrook School children, 1922.
Left to right: Back row: Fred Cashmore, Ted Rotherham, Claud Gill, Cyril Ison, Bill Hazel, Mrs Brian Dawkins (Headteacher, holding son Gerald)
Second row: Elsie Edkins, J Tallis, Connie Stone, Flo Moore, --- Cahmore, Ros Parnell, Louise Haycock, George Rotherham , Ella Reynolds.
Third row: Marjorie Loveridge, (?) , Bessie Sheppard, Grace Dawkins, (? , ----
Cashmore.
Front row:J Gosling, Frede Edkins, Herbert Edward Dick Parnell, Charles Loveridge, Fred Stone, ---- Goslins, Charlie Dawkins.

Copston Magna Church and old school, late 1950s. Copston School was built in 1847 by Lady Augusta Feilding, enlarged in 1912 and closed in 1949. It was used as the village hall until the mid-1960s. Clockwise: the cricket field; "The Hollies" garden, church and churchyard; school playground with chestnut trees, school house and garden, school garden.

Copston schoolchildren, 1944.
Left to right: back row: Derek Wood, Peter Arnold, (?) , Chris Rathbone, Joan Toone, David Toone. middle row: Michael Wood, John Arnold, Connie Hurrel, Miss Godridge, Angela Arnold, Sheila Lees, Harry Hibbert. front row: John Chappell, Helen Rose, Robin Toone, Donovan Toone, Roger Kind, Winnie Smith.

School Nativity Play, 1944, outside Copston Church.
Left to right: Shiela Lees (angel)
John Arnold, Connie Hurrel, (?) , (?) , Joan Toone, Peter Arnold, John Chapell
Roger Kind, Robin Toone, (?) , (?) , (?) , Winnie Smith, David Toone.

Christmas at Wolvey Primary School, 1998. The school in Bulkington Road now
provides primary education for over 200 pupils from the villages of Ansty, Burton
Hastings, Copston Magna, Shilton and Wolvey (including the military camp at
Bramcote).
Left to right: Gerald King (angel);
Liam Webb, Michael King, Aaron Carville, (?) , (?) , Matthew Ashley, Todd Lewis, (?);
Kristie Thorpe, Hannah Waters, Jill Hawcutt, Richard Lewis, (?) , Jonathan Robinson,
Brett Koenig;(?) .
Rori Cooper, Alicia Tudhope, Sam Wiggins, Jonathan Robinson, Brett Koenig;(?) ,
Ryan Ashmore, Holly Brittain, Pramila Limbu , (?) , Francesca Simmons.

Reunion of pupils of Wolvey School. Sixty pre-1946 pupils, their ages ranging from 50-84, met in the Wolvey Bowling Club in January 1997 with three former teachers. This was the third such event organised by John Whitehurst (far right, front row).

AGRICULTURE

The lighter soils of Wolvey Heath and Burton Hastings have meant that the area was attractive for farming from early times and there is evidence of Bronze Age activity in the area. Farming no doubt continued through Roman times. By 1086 there are records of arable and grazing associated with the a number of settlements in the area — Bramcote, Burton Hastings, Stretton Baskerville and Wolvey.

During the Middle Ages there were large open fields with grazing on the Heath. Evidence of the agriculture of these times can be seen in the ridges and furrows sometimes remaining in the fields. and from some farm names. Following the enclosures of the late eighteenth century, field boundaries became a characteristic of the English landscape and farmhouses were built by the fields. The intensive agriculture of the later twentieth century has removed some of these field boundaries.

River Anker Bridge, 1888. Working on the river bank, possibly preparing a place for stock to drink. Mr Weston (left) and William Wright.

Muck-spreading near Wolvey. Manure being spread on either allotments or fields, using only a wheelbarrow. Note that both men are smoking — perhaps their way of coping with the smell!

Jimmy Tompkins sharpening his scythe, 1950s. He left school at 14 to work for the Toone family at Copston and Highcross. Here he prepares to scythe his orchard at Little Wigston. A man could cut an acre of grass with a scythe in a day. At haymaking, a team of men were employed to mow a field.

Ploughing with a team of horses, Wolvey. In the centre is Jim Pheasant. Such a team could plough an acre in a day, the man walking eight miles. Today with modern machinery it is possible to plough twenty five acres in the same time.

Harrowing at Shelford. Bill Noon with his team of shires preparing the seedbed prior to sowing the grain.

Bill Noon of Shelford 'showing a leg'. He is sitting on a horse-drawn rake during haymaking, gathering the last of the hay.

Harvesting at Copston with a horse-drawn binder. In the background can be seen the shocks, a feature of cornfields before the combine harvester.

Harvesting at Copston, August 1938. A hay rake and a wagonette, pulled by two shire horses. Left to right: Mr Pratt, Ted Morphet, Joan Toone, Henton Toone, Reg Hibbitt, David Toone, Fred Toone, Cecil Hibbitt

Henton Toone with Captain, a prize winner at the Walsgrave Show, 1925. The wagon was built in 1866 and had many uses, including carrying cheese, sacks of coal and grain.

A fine shire owned by Colonel Atkins from Stretton Baskerville. He had a stud of prize winning stallions who were taken round the surrounding farms to serve their mares. Bill Bark senior is seen holding the horse at Poplar Lodge, close to Canal Bridge No 12.

Hunters at the stables of Colonel Atkins, Stretton House.
Left to right: (?) , Tom Sutton (Head Riding Groom), Betty Atkins (daughter), Colonel Jock Atkins, Bernard Thatcher (groom), Mrs Jock Atkins (neé Monica Standish), Dennis Hood (of Wolvey)

Mr Lew Russell of Shelford with his bull.   He was born in Coventry and came to Shelford in 1955 to farm a Warwickshire County Council small holding of 46 acres.

Fred Toone's herd of shorthorn cows returning to pasture after being milked at Copston. The church is behind the trees on the left.

Coventry Co-operative Milk Lorry, about 1918. Seen here at Little Wigston, the milk was fetched from a number of points along a route which included Wolvey and Withybrook. Prior to this most of the milk was converted into cheese which was stored to mature in cheese rooms in the farmhouses. It was taken to a cheese market in Leicester, in a wagon, twice a year.

One of the Stretton Baskerville flock of Shropshire sheep with Teddy Whickson. He was said never to take off his hat except when getting into bed, when it was put on the bedpost.

Barbara and Pam Lucas feeding their pet lamb, 'Mary Lamb', at their home, Ivy Cottage, Withybrook. Nearly every Spring there would be a cade (orphaned) lamb that needed to be fed, a task often taken on by country children.

Sheep in field by Cottage Farm, Cicey Lane, Burton Hastings, 1960s. The elm trees have now been removed and the field is occupied by bungalows.

The Hermitage, Wolvey Heath, 1891.
The small house was like many erected by a squatter on the Heath. It had walls of pebbly clay and straw and was surrounded by a small moat. It occupied the site of a Medieval hermitage. At the door are Mr and Mrs Veasey, the last of his family to live there 'since the hermits'. They are soon to leave the house as unfit for habitation. They would probably have had a few animals, the hay in the rick ready to feed them during the winter.

Sheering sheep at Copston, 1946. Henton Toone (right) in the yard at the Hollies Farm, Copston. Henry Rose is about to wrap the fleece.

Planting Potatoes at Burton Fields Farm, 1967-68. Left to right: Mabel Wilson, Stella Young, Ken Faulkner, Audrey Brandrick, Betty Faulkner.

Bert Clarke of Wolvey, world champion hedger, having a break. Examples of his superbly laid, stock-proof hedges were a feature of the countryside. He won the Young Farmer's competition for the best hedging work which was held on Joe Beale's farm in January 1953. The following year he won the Farmers' Weekly sponsored International Hedge-Laying Competition , which was also held in Wolvey on the Cope-Arnold's estate. In all he won this 10 times and together, no less than 155 championships.

Bert Morris on his first tractor, a standard Fordson. Note the metal wheels. Photographed at Bramcote Fields, 1940.

TRADE & INDUSTRY

In many ways the villagers were self-sufficient until well into the twentieth century. Both miller and blacksmith, essential to the farms, could be found in the villages; two mills are recorded in Burton Hastings as early as 1086. Wolvey, which tended to be the market centre, had a butcher and baker who served the area. As communications developed post offices were established at Burton Hastings, Withybrook and Wolvey.

Quite apart from having two major routes as a boundary to the area – Watling Street and the Fosse Way – the main road from Coventry to Leicester passed through the village of Wolvey. As a result there are a number of inns in the area and, with the advent of the motor car, garages. It was the repair of local roads by one local man with his steam roller that lead to the formation of the major civil engineering company, GallifordTry.

There were the usual cottage industries but in the late eighteenth and early nineteenth centuries, some of the cottagers were involved in both framework knitting of stockings – as an off-shoot of the well-known Hinckley industry – and in ribbon weaving – which had more affinities with the Coventry area.

Wolvey Windmill, 1904. The Templars are recorded as having a windmill and a water mill at Wolvey in 1308. This mill had been at Shepshed in Leicestershire until 1815 when it was dismantled, transported to Wolvey and reassembled. It was finally dismantled in 1909.

Wolvey Mill and Cottages. This mill was situated on Wolvey Heath at Mill Close. The Mill was used to produce flour and prepare animal feed. The house on the left was the home of Mr Riley, the church organist.

Burton Hastings Water Mill, 1950s. Here Percy Morris demonstrates how to carry an hundredweight sack of meal in the mill yard. He is accompanied by Joseph Freeman. In the 1930s, the mill was so busy that a queue of horses and carts loaded with grain would often stretch from the mill back to the canal bridge.

Burton Mill, 1962. Above, Jack Morris, the miller, is on the second floor, checking the flow of corn onto the stones. Below he is on the ground floor, filling the sacks with flour. His father, also a miller, first worked at the mill in 1888. There were two mills in Burton Hastings at the time of the Domesday Book.

The Old Smithy, Wolvey, 1899. The thatched smithy and cottage was burned down but the smithy continued on the same site, in front of the large chestnut tree. The Wrights were smiths for over 300 years. In the photograph (above) are John Wright as a young man (2nd right), John William Wright (father) was Blacksmith, Master Farrier and Wheelwright and carries a hammer. On extreme right: Joe Peacock and George Wright.

Blacksmithing Competition, Wolvey, 1950s. Joh n Wright (below) watches one of the competitors. He had won shoeing competitions in various parts of the country and came third at the Warwickshire Show when he was 82.

Blacksmithing Competitions, Wolvey, late 1920s. Officers, competitors and visitors pose in front of the Wolvey Smithy. The group include John Wright, Percy Toone, Mrs Toone, Miss Georgina and Mr Cranfield Coape-Arnold. Note the petrol pumps, an indicator of the future use of the site.

Withybrook Blacksmith, Mr Raymond Lucas. Outside his home , Ivy Cottage, with his wife Lucy, the school's infant teacher. With him are Mrs Gill and Ivy Hudson. Several generations of the Lucas family were blacksmiths (see photograph opposite).

Robert Furborough, Wolvey's Butcher (in apron).   He came to Wolvey aged 21 in 1899 and started business in Wolds Lane with £50. In 1903 he moved to a thatched house next to the Blue Pig. At an early stage he rented land at Fernhill Farm on Coventry Road where he built a slaughter house. He provided meat to the Coventry Wholesale Market as well as customers in Wolvey and the surrounding villages. With him (left to right) are: Freddie Knight, Leonard Yorke and Walter Moore.

Three Generations of the Lucas Family, 1904. William Lucas (centre) aquired the forge in Withybrook in 1888 and was village blacksmith until his death in 1921. His two sons, Frederick (left) and Raymond (opposite page) followed him, Raymond contiunuing until his death in 1960. On the right is William's father, John.

Butcher's Shop, Wolvey 1910. Mr Furborough outside his shop and home, next to the Blue Pig.

Butcher's Delivery Van, 1920s. Mr Furborough with his eldest son, Robert, by the van replacing the pony and trap which he had previously used to supply the adjoining villages. By this time the property had been completely rebuilt.

Mrs Elliott's General Store, Wolvey, before 1914. Known as 'open all hours', it was an agency for the Sketchley Dye Works. Before the 1914-18 War it was taken over by George Cox who changed it to a cycle shop. It was run by his wife Janet and sister Gertrude during the War. In 1921 the business moved to Coventry Road. The shop became a branch of the Co-op. Opposite can be seen the blacksmith. Further down the road were the Church and the Bull's Head. The only traffic on the road is a horse and cart.

Flagpole Cottage, Wolvey, 1930. Cissie Peppard stands in front of her sweet and newsagent's shop which was opposite the Bull's Head. In the window were bottles of sweets such as Humbugs. Inside were boxes of dolly mixtures and jelly babies. They all needed to be weighed out; as little as a ¼d could be spent. On Mondays and Thursdays the room on the opposite side of the front door served as the doctor's surgery. Patients waited in the hall.

Old Co-op Shop, Smithy and Bull's Head, Wolvey, 1927. The Burbage Co-operative Society started business in the village in 1918, moving into the corner shop in 1921. The manager, Joe Smith , at first lived with his wife over the shop. They later moved to Hinckley, the living accommodation becoming a drapery store.

The new Co-op Shop, built 1938. It had drapery, grocery and greengrocery departments. Joe Smith continued as manager until 1941, when he was tragically killed in an accident at the bottom of Temple Hill when cycling home. It was sold in the 1960s and today is the village's only shop.

Off licence, Wolvey. This was attached to the old bakehouse (the middle doorway) and was established by the Wright family in 1894. It was managed by George Wright and his daughter Gertrude until 1925. Since then there have been a number of tenants, the last being Victor (Vic) Wallis who took over in 1975. It closed finally in 1998.

The Square, Wolvey, 1930. Looking towards Wolds Lane, Mrs Minnie Watson's village stores is on the right. It started as a greengrocer's stall outside the "Beam Ends" cottage. In 1930 a shop was built which also stocked groceries, sweets and in the summer, home-made ice cream. Later the wooden shop was rebuilt in brick.. One of the two village pumps was in front of the shop. Next door is the Village Hall, built in memory of those who served in the First World War. Proposed in 1918, it was finally opened on 4 April 1920 at a cost of £1,119.

Old Post Office, Wolds Lane, Wolvey. The first postmaster was George Rowley in 1845. It was sited in several places until it moved here in 1908. From that date was served by three generations of the Cox family as postmaster. The last was Harold Cox who retired in 1967. This part of Wolds Lane was known as Post Office Road for a time. The Post Office Stores closed finally in 1998 and transferred to its present location on Church Hill.

Withybrook Post Office and Shop. When Mrs Howard, the postmistress retired in 1971 after 3½ years service, no replacement could be found. For many years the postmistress was Mrs Rotherham. The shop sold nearly everthing, with goods piled high on the counter, some even hanging from the ceiling. Everything had to be weighed out; the bacon was cut with a knife. At one time it had the village's only telephone. It was the source of all village information.

Burton Hastings Shop, 1950. From Mill Lane, looking towards Cecily Lane. As the village's sole shop it sold paraffin for the oil lamps before there was an electricity supply in Burton and at one time had the only telephone in the village to use in emergencies.

Burton Hastings Post Office. Mary Brandrick standing at the door of the village shop which was also the post office. Ethel Plowman is with her bicycle. The shop closed in 1987. A limited post office service continued in the front room of Cromwell House but this is now closed and there is no shop in the village.

The old Axe and Compass Inn, Moat Lane, Wolvey Heath, 1920. This is now a private house. There is a tradition that at one time it was the haunt of highwayman, Dick Turpin. In 1927 it was replaced by a new inn, built by Edgar Bailey who was responsible for building a number of houses in the village. Until its closure the fair granted by a Royal Charter in 1326 was held in a field opposite, on the Sunday closest to 6 July.

The Axe and Compass Inn at Five Ways, Wolvey Heath. The garage has been there since 1929. In the 1930s Mr Rees Lloyd, the owner, also ran a taxi service and his wife the Wolvey Heath Café. In the 1970s, following a number of serious accidents – this was the A46 Leicester to Coventry road – the large island was constructed.

The Bull's Head, Church Hill, Wolvey, 1920s. It was here, in October 1853, that Joseph Rowley, age 27, was killed in a brawl which led to Joseph Bolton spending four years in goal for his manslaughter. Here Church Hill is still quiet enough for children to play safely and even to learn to ride a bicycle. Len York, whose mother was licencee, ran a garage on the opposite side of the road. In the 1920s his bus provided much needed transport for the many villagers who worked in Hinckley. Prior to this they had to walk the four miles each way, whatever the weather.

The present Bull's Head Inn under construction. Both the old inn and a number of cottages were demolished to provide the car park. During construction the floor of the seventeenth century brewery malthouse was discovered – it used to supply five inns in the area. At that time the Bull's Head was known as the George and Dragon.

William Sewell, Licencee of the Blue Pig Inn, Wolvey, with his family, 1920s. Here they stand at the front door of the Inn, which, today, is still in its original building with a village pump on the forecourt. William Sewell was licencee for thirty years. Electricity was installed in 1928, probably the first of the inns to do so, because Mr Furborough , next door, included it in his scheme.

The Half Moon Inn from the approach to Withybrook from Rugby, c 1910. All Saint's Church is behind the trees on the right. During the 1930s, Mr Frank Dexter, the innkeeper, supplied the villagers with coal and paraffin. It was also the venue for the 'Sick & Divvy Club' supper. The Inn was sold for £8,600 to the Northampton Brewery in 1951.

The Half Moon Inn, Withybrook. Locals waiting on the bridge for opening time The name of the inn was changed to "The Pheasant" when it became a popular restaurant for people coming by car from nearby towns.

George Cox's Garage and Cycle Shop, Coventry Road, Wolvey, 1930s. He moved here from the Square in 1921. As motor traffic increased on the busy trunk road, he opened a garage to undertake motor car repairs.

Arthur Green's Garage, Coventry Road, Wolvey from the air, 1960. After he took over he concentrated on the motor trade and erected additional premises. Some time later the house was demolished and replaced by a bungalow. On the left is Fernhill Farm, its fields and orchard now occupied by housing.

Thomas John Galliford and family, 1922. Seen here with his wife, Edith, and two of their children, Dick and Jack. Mr Galliford was in partnership with Robert Furborough for a while, using their steam engines for ploughing and threshing.

The Galliford home, Leicester Road, Wolvey. It later became the home of the caretaker at the works before it was demolished in 1976 to make space for an extension to the offices. By now the company had international contracts.

Galliford's Steam Roller and Lorry, 1927-28.   During the 1920s the steam roller was used for road building work and was hired out to local authorities. With the death of Thomas Galliford and the departure of the sons on military service in 1939, the business was mothballed, although the rollers were used in the construction of the runways at Bramcote Aerodrome. With the return of Thomas William (Dick) and Walter George Galliford the business was reopened, the plant brought back to working order and supplemented with some wartime utility rollers. In 1952 the partnership became a private limited company.

Galliford's Skidpan, 1960. Situated next to the old cricket field, it was used for one of the special stages of the RAC International Rally. Crews came to Wolvey after completing a five lap race at Mallory Park. They then proceeded to Brands Hatch, avoiding the recently opened M1 motorway. Among the competitors was Pat Moss. It was also the first advanced driving school and featured on television, such personalities as Raymond Baxter visiting Wolvey for the purpose.

Galliford's Secretarial Staff. Peggy Galliford and the secretarial staff on the steps of the Galliford headquarters building, Wolvey. The number of staff reflect the growing size of the company. In 1964 they took part in a fashion parade in the village hall to raise money for its building fund.

Galliford Fleet of Lorries, 1960. Part of the fleet of tipper lorries used in the construction of the Coventry Inner Ring Road and the M1 motorway.

Well Sinking at Wolvey, 1890. Prior to the advent of mains water, possession of your own well saved journeys to the village pump. Thomas Allcoat (left) with his father (in bucket) brick-lining a well. Thomas Allcoat lived in Coventry Road and with abundant springs in the area, their skills were much in demand.

WAR AND PEACE

The rural scene and war seem incompatible. But the inhabitants of the area have experienced their share of armed conflict. The rout of Boudicca by the Romans in 61 AD took place not far away on Watling Street. Early in the fourteenth century, Sir Thomas Astley went with his retainers, many raised in Wolvey, to fight and die in Scotland at the battle of Bannockburn. Tradition has it that during the Civil War, Wolvey Hall was damaged during a skirmish with the Parliamentarians. The twentieth century has seen villagers serving, some dying, in the two world wars.

In 1939, the aerodrome was constructed at Bramcote, bringing with it far closer contact with the paraphernalia of war. Service personnel found their way into the social life of the area. Searchlights, "pill-boxes" and anti-aircraft guns appeared at strategic places, including Withybrook. A Home Guard was formed. The presence of service personnel at Bramcote has continued since then to this day, a period that has seen all three of the armed services in residence there at different times.

Steve Allen, Wolvey. In his First World War uniform (above) and as an old man (below). He was a village character and, like others who served in the First World War, his name is commemorated on the plaque in the Village Hall. In 1915 about a thousand Royal Fusiliers were billeted in Wolvey, some sleeping in the school.

Home Guard outside Wolvey Hall, 1944 (above)

Left to right:

Back row: Percy Knight, Eric Knight, Walter Moore, Joseph Taylor, John Webster, Ray Brown, Frederick Woodward, Bryan Elson, Gordon Brandrick, Dennis Bark, Joe Tipper, Rees Lloyd, Morris Chapman.

Next row standing: Thomas Martin, John Elson, William Ward, Leslie Reynolds, George Callington, Leonard York, George Bates, James Brophy, Ernest Carton, Robert Bourne, Anthony Moore, Ronald Kinchin, (?), James Chamberlain, Robert Dowsett.

Next row sitting: (?), John Williams, John Lovell, Mr Harold Bennett, Colonel, Mr Rodney Davis, Mr Reginald Bennett, Sid Sewell, Joseph Beale, Charles Wrightham, Reginald Elson.

Front row:

Reginald York, Henry Watson, Ernest Manton, (?), Bernard Thorpe, Sidney Mott.

Home Guard, 1940. Four members of the Toone family pictured on the Green at Copston Magna:

Left to right: Henton Toone, Parker Toone, Percy Toone and Joe Beale

Stanley Ward, Wolvey. (left) He served with the Royal Artillery in North Africa and Italy. He was the first to return home in Wolvey at the end of the war and had been away so long that his daughter did not know him. Note the tape on the windows to prevent flying glass, if bombed.

Wedding of Sergeant Donovan Toone to Enid Goodwin. A wartime marriage by special licence at Copston Church in September 1939. Donovan Toone joined the RAF Volunteer Reserve in 1938. He was promoted to Flight Sergeant and then commissioned as a pilot. In 1941 as a flight lieutenant in the Night Fighter Squadron he had his first success. He continued with them until February 1943 when he lost his life flying for his country.

King George VI at Bramcote, 1940. With the wartime Polish leader. General Sikorski, he inspected a parade of Polish airmen. The building of the aerodrome started in 1936 with the demolition of farmhouses, cottages and Wolvershill Hall.

Polish Airmen on Parade, 1940. The control tower has been camouflaged. These airmen went on to join bomber squadrons at RAF Swinderby. For a short period before their arrival, the entire fleet of Imperial Airways (later to become BOAC and British Airways) was at Bramcote.

HMS Gamecock, Bramcote, 1949.   Crash of a Royal Naval Air ServiceFirefly, Mark 1. The Royal Navy took over from the Royal Air Force at Bramcote in 1946, after which the aerodrome was run as a ship.

Sailors in front of Hanger No 3, Bramcote. With the development of new aircraft, the runway was no longer suitable and the Royal Navy left Bramcote in 1958.

Junior Leaders Regiment, Royal Artillery. The Regiment moved into Bramcote in 1959. Their training included regular distance running and it became a familiar sight to see young soldiers on the roads of Wolvey and Burton Hastings. The Regiment was accorded the Freedom of Nuneaton and here (left) they are exercising their right to march through the town with fixed bayonets and drums beating.

Corporal Tulasi Rai, Gurkha Piper, Royal Corps of Signals. A batallion of Gurkha troops form part of the 30th Regiment of the Royal Corps of Signals, now at Bramcote. The children receive their primary education at Wolvey School where this photograph was taken. Left to right: Lucy Haywood and Rostani Ranu standing; Suvechna Gurung and Michael William, seated.

Mrs Jude, Evacuees' School Mistress. Early in the Second World War a number of evacuees came from the east end of London with their teacher, Mrs Jude, to lodge with families in Withybrook. The children had their lessons in the Village Hall. They called their teacher "Punch and Judy". After the Coventry Blitz, farmers let displaced families have their spare rooms. The workers had to walk to Shilton each day for transport to take them into Coventry.

Sinney Fields Cottage, Burton Hastings (above) was used to house German and Italian POWs under the supervision of War Agricultural Staff. Now demolished, it had many years earlier been the home of Albert and Mary Morris, before thay moved to the Mill.

Helmut, a German Prisoner of War at Withybrook (right). He came each day from the POW camp at Pailton to work with Mr Lucas, the blacksmith. In the winter of 1947, POWs dug through the snow so that the milk could be collected.

Wolvey British Legion outing to Wickstead Park, 1950. Members with their wives and children on a visit to the Park. Also a popular venue for Sunday School outings from all the villages. The café served fish paste sandwiches, jelly icecream and cake.

Wolvey British Legion's New Standard, 1950.
The branch was officially opened in March 1950 at a meeting in the Village Hall attended by visitors from surrounding branches. The President was Mr Len York and the Secretary Mr Ernie Allen. In the photograph from left to right: Joe Moore (holding flag), Joe Hood, Henry Watson, Jack Wright, Lou England, Ernie Allen, Len York, Jack Williams, Reg Moore.

Wolvey British Legion, October 1950. Members marching to church for the dedication of their standard. The parade was led by a Royal Marines band from RNAS Bramcote, with both the county and Wolvey standard flying. The previous evening 180 members and friends attended a dinner in the Village Hall, followed by musical entertainment.

VJ Day Anniversary Celebrations, Wolvey, 1995. The fiftieth anniversary of the cessation of war with Japan in 1945 was celebrated with a procession, tea for adults in the Village Hall and a street party for the children in The Square. Visitors from neighbouring towns and villages mingled with the villagers.

Exhibition of Wartime Memorabilia, Wolvey. Arranged in the small room of the Village Hall, here being admired by Ernie Allen, an ex-serviceman and member of the Local History Group who mounted the exhibition, organised by Mrs Eileen Bassnett

Desmond Lamb of Wolvey. Pictured here with his great-niece, Emmalene Gale, a Coventry schoolgirl, they represented the youth and ex-servicemen of England in a VE anniversary celebration in the presence of Queen Elizabeth, the Queen Mother. He was one of two prisoners of war living in Wolvey, the other being Frank Middleton.

EVENTS & CELEBRATIONS

Smaller communities have a greater interest in the happenings around them. Here we record some personal and family events like weddings, or a traffic accident which involved strangers.

On the other hand the arrival of mains services like electricity and water involved the whole area, changed habits of a lifetime and were important events in the history of the villages.

It is perhaps a heightened community spirit that particularly leads to the recognition of national events and which the villagers have celebrated in their own way over the years.

Bride and Father on their way to the Wedding. Sheila Malin married Ken Pardoe at Wolvey Baptist Chapel on 7 August 1970. Here, on their way to the Chapel they pass cottages on both sides which had been demolished by 1978. At the end of the path a cottage in Wolds Lane has its thatch protected by corrugated iron sheeting.

The wedding of Mary (Polly) Moore and Jake Lines, Wolvey.

Left to right: front row: Betsy Lavinia Moore, (?), (?), Ida Bageley, Ellen Letitia Lizzie Brown; Middle row: (?), (?), Alice Moore, Jake Lines, Mary (Polly) Moore, Walter Moore, Mercy Wright; back Row: George York is in the centre.

Burton Hastings Wedding, 1926. John (Jack) William Wright and Ellen Florence Parsonage married on 27 January, 1926. Left to right: back: Marguerite Parsonage, Walter Wright (Best Man) the Bridegoom, Mr & Mrs Harry Parsonage; front: Peggy Hodgeson (later Mrs Galliford), Mabel Liggins, the Bride, Eadie Parsonage.

Withybrook marriage, 1895. The wedding of Seaman Austin Woods . Left to right:back row: Mr Ted Eversden, M Lucas; front row: Mrs Woods, Leah Eversden, Bridegroom, Bride, Alice Eversden, Miss Wall. Two brothers of Leah Eversden were killed in the Great War.

Wedding of Amanda Furborough and Carl Beck, Wolvey, 10 June1935. On the lawns of Wolvey Vicarage, Left to right: Muriel Beck, Douglas Edgar (Bestman), Mrs Beck (Groom's mother), Carl and Amanda Beck, Robert and Alice Furborough (Bride's parents), Noreen York (cousin & bridesmaid), Rev Stanley Morris. Seated: Margaret & Alison Furborough (sisters), Betty & Shirley Furborough (nieces).

Wedding Reception prepared for Doris (née Hardy) & Tom Smith, Burton Hastings. The school room set out for the wedding reception. With no village hall or public house, this was the only place such events could occur.

Sheila & Roy Elliott leaving their Wedding Reception, Wolvey, 1958. Sheila was the villages' district nurse and Roy a Burton Hastings famer and the Baptist Chapel organist. The reception was held at the Village Hall - note the windows and door on the front of the Hall.

Carrying Water with a Yoke, Wolvey. (left) Mr Malin, carrying buckets of water from the well, using a yoke. He is with his mother. Mains water only reached the villages after the Second World War.

John Hurley pumping water for the last time, Wolvey, 1956. (right) Here he pumps water from the pump in The Square. The other pump survives outside the Blue Pig, although the water is condemned as being unfit to drink. Mains water was installed at Wolvey in 1956.

House on Fire in Hall Lane, Wolvey, 1920s. (below) The crowd of spectators indicates how many villagers were around to watch the firemen, unlike today when the majority commute elsewhere each day. Fire was an ever present risk with so many houses having thatched roofs. During the war many of the roofs were covered with corrugated iron or asbestos sheeting to protect them from incendiary bombs.

Pump next to the School, Burton Hastings. This was one of the villages two pumps. The installation of mains water started in April 1954 at a cost of "£26,000.

Early Car Crash, Wolvey, 1920. An open-topped charabanc (coach) and car in collision on the Coventry Road by the garden of Bachelor's Rest. Being the main road from Coventry to Leicester as well as the trunk route from Bath to Lincoln (A46) meant increasing volumes of traffic and of accidents until the M69 was fully opened in 1977. The continuous flow of traffic effectively divided the village into two. Even in the days before motor vehicles there is a record of a road accident on Temple Hill which resulted in the death of a lion from Lord John Sanger's circus.

General Election, 1910. The candidate's Humber car provides an attraction in Wold's Lane for Wolvey's children. A motor car was a novelty when walking or riding a horse were the main means of transport. Thirty years later during the Second World War when petrol rationing was in force, horse-drawn traps were used again; those parked in the Bull's Head car park used to attract attention from the children.

Village Outing, Withybrook, 1920s. Two charabancs and over 60 villagers pose in the main street, something impossible with today's traffic. They are dressed in their Sunday-best clothes. The elderly man on the far left is Ted Payne, who was in the building trade.

Coronation Day, Wolvey, 1953. Florie Wright's cottage in Post Office Road (now corner of Wolds Lane and Croft Close) decorated for the occasion. On that day the village awoke at 7.00 am to a royal salute fired by members of the British Legion. At 9.00 am there was a short church service. Many watched the coronation on television, either with friends or on their first set, bought for the occasion. At 2.00 pm the celebrations included a sports programme, a fancy dress event and then an excellent meal for 700 adults and children. Heavy rain prevented the firework display and bonfire which was held the next day. However, free drinks and dancing wound up the festivities. The village gained two bus shelters to commemorate the occasion.

Fancy Dress Parade, Wolvey Conservative Fête, October 1949 (below). The fête was held at Wolvey Hall and attractions included a steam train, clairvoyant, Spinning Jenny and dance music by the Rythem Boys. Left to right: Mary Burbage, Margaret Perkins, Mary Middleton (with big hat), Janice Pheasant, Jane Barratt (fairy), Ann Smithengale, Sarah Davis.

Garden Fête, Wolvey Grange, 1934. The event is being opened on the lawns at the home of auctioneer, Mr Percy Toone. Attractions would have included the Foden's Motor Works Band, games such as skittles and guessing the weight of a pig.

Wolvey Carnival Float 'Oliver Twist', 1991. The procession of floats was led by the Carnival Queen and her Maids of Honour riding on top of Galliford's horse-drawn bus. Their destination, after processing through the village, was the Playing Field.

Choral Society float, Wolvey Carnival, 1991. They depict the Cries of London. The carnival ended at the playing field with races, a dog obedience competition and a number of stalls. Left to right: Colin Napman, Margaret Howles, Frank Middleton, George Williams, June Spencer, Yvonne Thorpe.

PEOPLE & ORGANISATIONS

We have only limited knowledge of the people and organisations in the area up to the nineteenth century. Most of this concerns land-owners and the church.

With the advent of photography we begin to find an often uncon-scious record of a much wider spectrum of village life. The Group's photographic archive enables us to catch a glimpse of the people in the villages, and their organisations which have contributed so much over the last hundred years.

Mr Cranfield Coe Henry Coape-Arnold, JP (1874-1963). Mr Coape-Arnold of Wolvey Hall and Farm outside Arnswell. He was a member of the Rugby Rural District Council and a farmer in Wolvey. He continued to use horses on the farm long after tractors had come into use. However, he used modern techniques in developing a piggery for some 300 animals.

Mr and Mrs Joseph Parker Toone, 1890. Here they are sitting in their garden at Highcross. Behind them is the monument erected by the Earl of Denbigh and other landowners in 1712 to mark the crossing of the two Roman roads – Watling Street and Fosse Way. Mr Toone farmed in Copston and at Highcross until 1932. He attended the meet of the Atherstone Hunt and was mounted when he was aged 90.

Mr George Wright, the baker, with pony and trap, Wolvey. He came to Wolvey in 1894 with his son, Osborne, and daughter, Moll, and had a bakehouse in Wolds Lane next door to the Off-licence. The pony and trap were used to deliver bread to Bramcote and Smockington. He was succeeded by Albert Sawford in 1922.

Mr Albert Allcoat's Rover car. Mr Allcoat was the greengrocer in Wolvey and lived at Bachelor's Rest. With his "old faithful", 1904 Rover car he toured Wales, taking great pride that it could cope with all the high passes. Despite many offers, he kept the car until his death in 1971.

Thomas Ward of Wolvey with his wife, Harriet and son Stanley, 1911. (left) He had a single storey, lean-to shop on Wolds Lane in 1914 where he sold and repaired Triumph and Singer motorcycles. He also worked at Sketchley Dye Works.

Robert Furbrough and Mrs Lizzie Peacock in Coventry Road, Wolvey, 1930s. (right) When there was a death in the village, Mrs Peacock would be summoned to 'lay out the corpse'. The coffin would be made by Thomas Rose, the village joiner and wheelwright. The bier, now in the church, was used to carry the coffin to church or chapel.

Some of the Staff at Wolvey Hall, 9 October 1924. (left) The Hall and Farm was a major employer in the village. In 1963, seven men were employed on the farm.

Nurse Elizabeth Callison Hall, September 1939. She came to Wolvey in 1921 as a private nurse and stayed on as district nurse and midwife, employed by the Nursing Association and subsequently the NHS until her retirement in 1953. She never learned to drive and in consequence used her bicycle for visits to the surrounding villages. In the photograph are, left to right: Ida Moore and Nurse Hall (back row) with June Moore, Nora Ward (with baby Angela), Betty Furborough.

Ann Ward, at the door of her home, 1900. When she married John Ward, she signed her marraige certificate with a cross. Like many of her generation she had never learned to write.

Church Lane, Wolvey, 1900. These cottages were the homes of Roseanne and Jim Pheasant, Ted Joyce, Bill and Ida Moore. It was later known as School Lane.

Bachelor's Rest. The cottage on the corner of Bulkington Road and The Square, contained a collection of antiques, including a large music box that played for an old penny, and a tuba that had belonged to Wolvey's brass band. The beautiful, much photographed garden, has a number of staddle stones. The crowd on the left are watching a parachute display, visible above the cottage roof.

Dr James Balfe, Wolvey's Doctor. Here he is talking to Rev. Gibbons and his wife. He joined the practice of Dr O'Donavan in 1943 and retired, as senior partner, in 1980. At first there was a consulting room in the front room of Flagpole Cottage, but this later moved to the Village Hall. Examinations had to be conducted at the main surgery at Burbage. A surgery was opened on The Square in 2002.

Ted Joyce and Jim Poynton with their paintings. This display was arranged for a meeting of the Darby and Joan Club. Ted Joyce (left) holds his painting of the old Axe and Compass Inn. A keen local historian, and the Local History Group's first president, he enjoyed painting the villages as he remembered them. Tim Poynton preferred to paint animals. He worked in the car industry.

Presentation to Dick Hollick, September 1978. Despite being confined to a wheel chair as the result of a flying accident, he was founder and secretary of the Wolvey Playing Fields Trust. The presentation is being made by Mrs Kate Davis, MBE, JP, of the White House, Wolvey, who was for many years Chairman of the Parish Council. Her award was in recognition of her service to the local community.

Leaving Burton Hastings Church. Left to right: Mrs Winifred Toone, Mrs Middleton (school teacher), Mrs Wells (Headteacher), Mrs Madge Callington, Rev Hudson, Mrs Elizabeth Chamberlain, Mr Ward (Churchwarden), Mrs Plowman (Church caretaker), Mrs Ada Allen, Hilton Wilson.

Christine Thompson with her Parents. She lived most of her life in this cottage by Anker Bridge, Bramcote. During the war she worked at the aerodrome. She was an active member of the Conservative Association and of the Local History Group. She kept geese to warn her of intruders.

Caroline Ann Harrad. Born in 1856, she spent her childhood in Burton Hastings where she was taught in the Old School House. At the age of 29 she married John Reynolds, a trimmer, and moved to Hinckley.

Jim and Elizabeth Morris, Burton Hastings. He was a miller, first at Tuttlehill Windmill in Nuneaton and then at Bilston Mill, Leicestershire. They lived at The Elms, Cicey Lane in retirement.

Three generations in the Rick Yard at Burton Mill, 1962 (left) . Mary Morris (with stick), Stella Young, Shirley Young (now Bower) with Paddy.

Burton Hastings Womens Institute. Mrs Ada Allen, Mrs Else Lowe and Mrs Annie Plowman (right) on a trip to Blackpool

Mrs Gladys Tongue of Withybrook with her floral exhibit which won the Huxley Cup at the Royal Show, July 1975. She lived in the old post office and grew most of the flowers for her arrangements in her own garden.

William and Catherine Lucas with baby Frederick John, 1890. He was Withybrook's blacksmith from 1888-1921 and was succeeed by another son, Raymond, who retired in 1960.

The Lucas Children outside Ivy Cottage, Withybrook, 1907. Left to right (with year of birth): Frederick (1889), Dorothy (1891), Gertrude (1893), Phyllis (1894), Raymond and Florence (twins 1896), Bentman (1898), Walter (1900), Gladys (1903) and Catherine (1906)

Mrs Lily May Pretona Clark with her dog, Lizzie. She was mother of the champion hedgers, helped on the farm and was much involved in village activities. Here she is preparing for the best kept village competition.

Withybrook's Champion Hedgers. Bert, Ron, Alan and George Clark. Bert was international champion, George and Alan won first and second prizes in the under 25s class. In 1956 and 1957, Ron won first prize when only 14 years old.

Flower Festival, Withybrook Church, 1989. Here Morris Woodward, church warden, brings in vital water supplies to quench the thirst of the participants.

Wolvey Young Farmers, 1983. Established in 1945, they hold fortnightly meetings with lectures and quizzes on farming and rural life. Social activities included dances and whist drives; in the summer visits are made to farms and shows. Here the cast of 'Oh! Really Vicar', performed as part of Bullocks, their entry into the National Young Farmers Drama and Entertainment Competition. The back row (left to right) includes: John Wells (with guitar), Sue Ensor, Alan Spencer, David Woodward, Michael Alton, Fre Semple (with guitar); front row: Mary Smith, Paul Summers, Andrea Ibbetson, Mary Moore, Neil Fletcher.

Wolvey Choral Society Review: Mary Middleton and Yvonne Thorpe. Successful musicals were among the entertainments produced for the older residents of the village.

Members of the Wolvey Choral Society with their Conductor, Bill Malin, 1958. (above)
Left to right:
Front row: Freda Mac (née Hood), Diane Bark, Jill Beasley (née Sewell), Sandra Warwick (née Malin), Betty Compton, Angela Ward, Betty Willis.
Second row: Mabel Green, Stella Hughes, Phyllis Bark (Payne), Ivy Thorpe (Hurley), Edie Baylis, Bessie Compton, Ruby Malin (Rowley), Sheila Malin (Pardoe), Mrs Ball , Sheila Elliott.
Standing: Roy Elliott, Florie Wright, Charlie Tompkinson, Sheila Elliott, Eunice Elliott, Frank Middleton, Eunice Middleton, Muriel Allen, John Green, Peter Grinham, Bill Malin (Conductor), (?), Yvonne Thorpe, Sid Sewell, Jessie Leamont, Wendy Hood, Vi Shilton, Dick Kinchin, John Shilton.

The Choral Society was formed soon after the opening of the Village Hall in 1919. One of the founder members was William Lines, leader of the village band. Their first conductor was Edwin Newcombe of Barnacle. The Society fell into abeyance and was refounded 1942-45 to raise funds for the families of those in the services in Wolvey. After the War it continued to raise funds for the 'Old Folk's Tea', as it was affectionately known.

Darby and Joan Easter Bonnet Parade, 1984
Left to right:
Front row: (?), Florence Morley, Florence Wright, Edith Brown, (?), Joan Caldicote, Lou Hall.
Back row: Jean Thorpe, Connie Milner, (?), (?), Mrs Jackson, (?), Ida Moore, Florence Martin, Sheila Yap, Kath Miller.

Wolvey Local History Group, 1986.   The launching of their first booklet on the history of Wolvey. This took place at the Blue Pig Inn in medieval style with suckling pig on the menu.   Dennis Briant, one of the founders of the Group and for many years its chairman is standing third from the left.

Wolvey Local History Group visit.   Visits are a regular feature of the Group's programme. Here members are enjoying Baddesley Clinton. left to right: Joan Toone, Eric Bordoli, Geoff Lewis, Jennifer Burton, David Alford, Norman Butler, Kath Butler, Frances Lewis, Anne Toone.

Burton Mill visit, 1993. Nigel Bower showing members of the Local History Group around the Mill. Left to right: John Fletcher, Nigel Bower, Kath Butler, Stanley Woodward (who was the Group's archive specialist).

Wolvey and Burton Hastings Womens Institute, 1977. Members planting a tree at the Playing Field to celebrate the silver jubilee of Queen Elizabeth II. The Institute was founded in 1943 and has regular meetings in the Village Hall. Left to right: (?), Ann Longdon, Eileen Hollick, Pal Warner, Hilda Bark, Nora Ward, Sheila Elliott, Pat Wooley, Dorothy Lloyd, Sandra Stanley, Jackie Bailey.

Womens Institute Pantomime, 1998. (above) This performance of Cinderella raised money for the Wolvey Church millennium project and new curtains for the Wolvey Village Hall stage. The stars and principals were (left to right) back row: Judith Penman, Ann Brandrick, Yvonne Thorpe, Glenys Ensor & Eileen Hollick (cow), Eleanor Locket (goose), Sheila Elliott. Front row: Joan Unett, Sandra Horsley, Lynne Hunt, Sue Ensor, Mary Holt.

Withybrook Womens Institute, 1969. Cutting the birthday cake. Left to right: Mrs E Graham (Vice President), Mrs E McGhee (who iced the cake), Mrs D Draper (President), Mrs E Dewes (Vice President, who made the cake).

Withybrook Womens Institute, 1963. Visit to Wedgwood potteries. Such outings are a regular activity and on one ocassion included a visit to France. Left to right: back row: Mrs D Collett, Mrs M Gill, Mrs Smith, Mrs Y Rotherham, Miss W Lucas, Mrs E Bloor. middle row: Mrs Jenson, (?), (?), Mrs H Hudson, Miss Avis Holt, Mrs N Gill, (?). bottom row: (?), (?), Mrs Clark, Mrs A Holt, Mrs Woodward, Mrs R Franklin, Mrs E Dewes, Mrs G Rotherham.

SPORTS & ENTERTAINMENT

It is difficult to conceive, in an age of television, leisure and recrea-
tion, how our forebears passed their spare time. Certainly the working week was much longer, and in the absence of electricity and
gas, and labour-saving devices, the day would have been differently
ordered. Ball games go back into antiquity and, for example, Mano-
rial rolls refer to fines for bowling when able men should have been
practising archery - then regarded as military training. However, for
the last hundred years there is a wealth of photographs illustrating
how the villagers occupied some of their free time.

Skating on the Ashby Canal, Burton Hastings, 1980s. During cold winters when the canal froze it was possible to skate, as Douglas Brandrick (left) and Nigel Bower are here. Today, with warmer winters and ice-breaking barges to keep the canal navigable, this is not now possible.

Ashby Canal, Burton Hastings, 1950s. When the canal fell into disuse it was used for fishing and sometimes swimming in the summer. The increased popularity of canal holidays has now reduced such activity.

Old Cricket Field and Pavilion, Wolvey. The field below the church used to serve as the cricket field, giving a typical English village scene on the approach from Leicester. On one occasion during a match, the ball was hit through the window of a Midland Red double-decker bus! The Wolvey Cricket Club was founded in 1914 and this ground was loaned to the Club by Mr Percy Toone in 1922.

Wolvey Cricket Team, 1973.
Left to right: back row: John Spillane, Bill Moore, Richard Smith, David Moore,David Wrightham, Brian Lewis, David Eglin (umpire). front row: Hilton Wilson, Roy Boffey, Francis Wright, David Woodward, John Wright.

Cup won by Wolvey Football Team, 1952. Jack Wright (chairman) holding the cup. In the final they beat Meriden Rovers 5-1. Left to right: Joe Moore, Colin Hood, Brian Morley, David Thorpe, Fred Hood.

Wolvey British Legion Football Club, May 1952. Founded in 1951, they won the Major Boyd Carpenter Cup the following year. Left to right: front row: Doug Thorpe, Brian Ellsworth, Leslie Jackson, Allan Wiggins, John Hurley. middle row: Jack Copeland, John Whitehurst, Arthur Green, Hedley Knight, Francis Cook, Fisher. back row: Joe Hood, Jack Williams, Eric Middleton, Jack Wright, Jim Brophy, Joe Moore, Len York, Dick Kinchen, Bill Sparks, George Bates, Basher

Wolvey Bowling Club, 1920s. A group of members shortly after the Club was founded. Initially they played on the lawn at Wolvey Grange. The new pavilion on the Club's present site was erected in 1939.

Wolvey Ladies Bowling Team, 1956. The successful team that won the News Chronicle National Club Tournament, in which over a thousand clubs entered. Included in the photograph are Priscilla Coleman and Audrey Evans (back row) with Joe Arnold, Dick Bailey, Mrs Bailey, Mrs Hackney and Mrs P Toone. The Ladies Team was founded in 1939.

Wolvey Hockey Team, 1930s. *They played teams from Nuneaton and Hinckley and in 1939 beat Hinckley Technical College 9-1.*
Left to right: back row: Enid Goodwin, Beryl Thorpe, Margaret Meadows, Kathleen Allcoat, Stella Bailey. front row: Mary Coley, Dinah Coley, Van Woodward, Janet Milner, Grace Thorpe, Betty Plumber.

Croquet on the Lawn, 1870. *Here John Toone relaxes with his family from a game of croquet at High Cross. He had eight children. Four of the children died young. The remaining four (2 sons and 2daughters) were engaged and married within eighteen months of each other and all lived to celebrate their golden weddings.*

Sunday Afternoon Rabbiting, 1910. Ferrets were used to catch rabbits. Most farmers were glad to be rid of rabbits because of the damage they caused to their crops. The rabbits caught provided a tasty and free source of meat. Included in the photograph are Bert Howe and Tony Pepper.

Atherstone Hunt meeting, The Square, Wolvey, circa 1910. The hunting season was from November to the end of March. This view is looking towards Church Hill with the Smithy on the right. Note the lady riding side-saddle.

Hunt meeting, Burton Hastings. Here the Hunt is assembling on The Green, outside Grove Farm.

Master Royston flying Bramcote Brook, 1904. The lime tree in the background is still there today.

Run to Earth near Cloudsley Bush, 1904. The hunt took place over Lord Denbigh's Newnham Padox estate which included all the land in the parish of Copston.

Atherstone Hunt Point to Point, 1951. George Callington riding Burton Boy, whose stable name was Flicker.

Point to Point Races, 1904. Meeting by Burton Lane, the traps and carriages were used to give the spectators a better view of the riders and horses.

Wolvey Dance Band, 1930.
During the 1920s and 30s Sid Sewell led the band in dances in all the surrounding villages. A ticket for one of the dances cost one shilling and sixpence (7½p). In 1927 the band led a charleston competition at the Burbage Co-Op Hall. Left to right: standing: George Gardner (Shilton), John Cope (Wolvey Heath). sitting: Johnson (Wolvey Hall), Ida Sewell (Wolvey), Joseph Allcoat (Wolvey), Sid Sewell (Wolvey).

Wolvey British Legion Dominoes Team, 1951. They represented Warwickshire in the quarter and semi finals of the Midland Indoor Games Tournament, which they won, but lost in the finals at Shrewsbury.

Left to right: standing: Lew England, Phil Snell, Frank Elson, Les Moore.

sitting: Harry Crowe, Jack Brown, Doug Thorpe, Gordon Bark, Jim Brophy.

ACKNOWLEDGMENTS

This work is based on the Group's collection of photographs which has been made over a number of years and involves a large number of photographers and sources. We are grateful to all who have contributed to this and trust that we have acknowledged them in the list that follows. If there is an omission we apologise and on hearing of it will gladly rectify it in any subsequent editions of this book..

W B Addison, Mavis Addison, Betty Bark, John Baxter & Sons, *Bedworth Echo*, Birmingham Central Library, John Bland, B Boffey, Margaret Bordoli, Shirley Bower, Ann Brandrick, Stan & Margaret Brandrick, Reg Bull, John Burton, Mr & Mrs P Callington, Jim Chamberlain, *Coventry Evening Telegraph, Coventry Standard*, Betty Faulkner, Teresa Fletcher, Mary Freeman, Peter Galliford, Peggy Galliford, GallifordTry plc, Jean Gordon, Arthur Green, *Heartland Evening News, Hinckley Times,* Eileen Holick, Bert Howe, Ivy Hurley, Lois Joyce, Mrs King, Desmond Lamb, Dorothy Lloyd, Mr Malin, John McNaughton, P Metcalf, Frank Middleton, Dianne Moore, Mrs P Morris, Percy Morris, Mrs Myring, *Nuneaton Tribune,* R R Panler, John Parfitt, Les Reynolds, Sid Sewell, Sid Sewell's daughter, John Slee, Jill Smith, Angela Taylor, John Thorpe, Wilma Thorpe, Yvonne Thorpe, David Toone, Joan Toone, Helen Trivet, Alan Warner, Joseph Watson, Chris Wilson, Hilton Wilson, Stanley Woodward collection, Jack Wright, Peter Wright, Doris York, Stella Young.